You can Save the Planet

Down the Drain: Conserving Water

Chris Oxlade and Anita Ganeri

Heinemann Library
Chicago, Illinois

© 2005 Heinemann Library,
a division of Reed Elsevier, Inc.
Chicago, Illinois

Customer Service 888-454-2279
Visit our website at www.heinemannlibrary.com

Designed by Richard Parker and Q2A Solutions
Illustrations by Q2A and Jeff Edwards
Photo research by Maria Joannou and Virginia Stroud-Lewis
Printed in China by WKT Company Limited

09 08 07 06 05
10 9 8 7 6 5 4 3 2 1

Library of Congress Cataloging-in-Publication Data
Ganeri, Anita, 1961-
    Down the drain : conserving water / Anita Ganeri and Chris Oxlade.-- 1st ed.
        p. cm. -- (You can save the planet)
Includes bibliographical references and index.
ISBN 1-4034-6845-1 (hc, library binding) -- ISBN 1-4034-6851-6 (pb)
1. Water conservation--Juvenile literature. I. Oxlade, Chris. II.
Title. III. Series.
    TD388.G36 2005
    333.91'16--dc22
                                        2004020667

Acknowledgments
The author and publishers are grateful to the following for permission to reproduce copyright material:
pp.4, 17, 19, 20, 21 Tudor Photography; p. 5 Michael S. Yamashita/Corbis; p. 7 Rex Features; p. 8 Gareth Boden; p. 9 Corbis; p. 11 Stone/Getty Images; p. 12 Colin Cuthbert/Science Photo Library; p. 13 Mark Boulton/ICCE; p. 14 Ginny Stroud-Lewis; p. 15 Anna Clopet/Corbis; p. 16 Johnny Buzzerio/Corbis; p. 18 Dk Images; p. 22 Still Pictures; p. 23 Alamy; p. 24 Dr Gopal Murti/Science Photo Library; p. 25 Mike McQueen/Impact; p. 26 Dr Jeremy Burgess/Science Photo Library; p. 27 Bridgeman Art Library.

Cover photograph by Alamy/The Photolibrary Wales.

Every effort has been made to contact copyright holders of any material reproduced in this book. Any omissions will be rectified in subsequent printings if notice is given to the publishers.

contents

Some words are shown in bold, **like this**. You can find out what they mean by looking in the glossary.

Why Do We Need Water?

Water is vital for our lives. Every plant, animal, and person needs water to grow and stay alive. Water is also an important **resource**. We use it for washing, cleaning, cooking, and drinking. Farmers use it for growing **crops** and raising animals, and factories need it for making things.

Science Behind It: Drinking Water

Two-thirds of your body is made of water. You lose water when you breathe out, sweat, and urinate. To replace all the lost water, you need to drink about two quarts (two liters) of water every day. You need more if you are playing sports or are out in hot weather. You could stay alive for more than a month without food, but you could only survive for a few days without water.

Water is the most important substance that we need to stay alive.

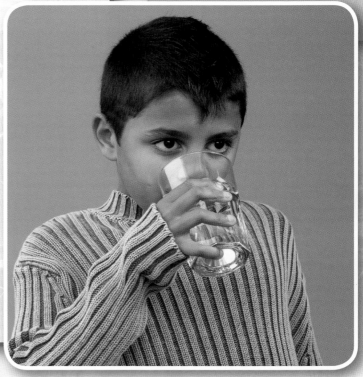

What is the problem?

Two-thirds of Earth is covered with water, but most of it is salty. Only one percent of all the Earth's water is freshwater that we can use. This means that water is a precious resource. Some places are very short of water, so it is important that we do not waste it. Instead we must save, or conserve, it. We must also keep water supplies clean, because dirty water can spread diseases and harm the people and animals that drink it.

4

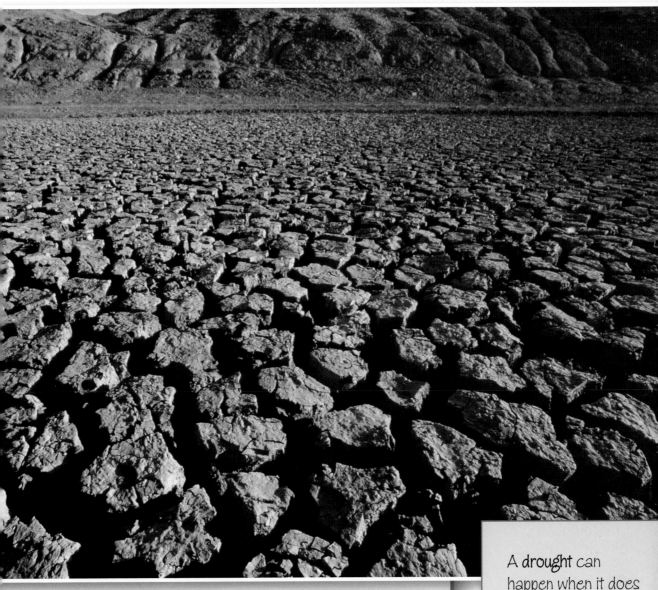

Taking Action: What Can I Do?

If we waste too much water, we will have problems finding enough water in the future. You might think that the problem is too big for you to do anything about. But if each of us does something, together we can make a big difference. Look for Taking Action boxes like this one throughout this book. They will give you ideas for action you can take to conserve water.

A **drought** can happen when it does not rain for months on end. Plants and animals may die without water.

Why should we conserve water?

Two-thirds of Earth is covered in water so you might think that there would be plenty of water to go round. But most of this water is in the oceans, and ocean water is salty. You cannot drink it because it would make you more thirsty, and sick, too. The salt also means we cannot use sea water for washing, cleaning, or growing plants. We need to conserve water, because there really is not that much we can use.

What water can we use?

The water that we can use is called freshwater. It does not contain salt. Only three percent of all the water on Earth is freshwater. Most of this is locked away as ice near the North Pole and South Pole and in glaciers on high mountains. The only water available for us to use is in rivers and lakes and under the ground in **aquifers**.

This chart shows where all the world's water resources are stored.

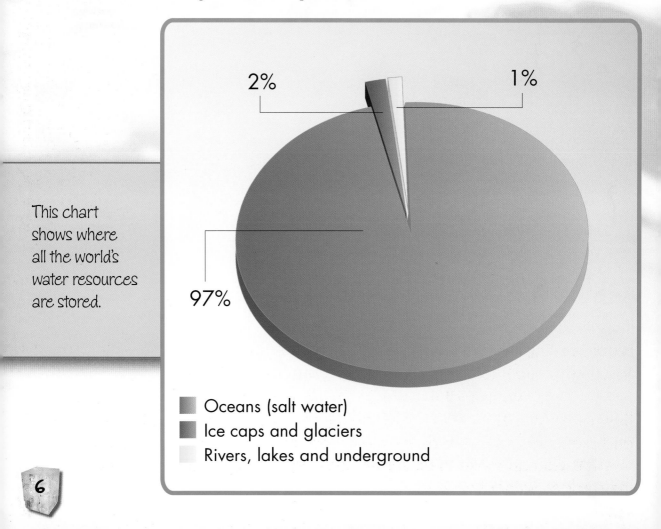

2%   1%

97%

■ Oceans (salt water)
■ Ice caps and glaciers
   Rivers, lakes and underground

What happens if we use too much water?

If some people use more water than they need, other people can be left short of water. For example, if people take too much water from one part of a river, there may not be enough water for people living farther downstream. If we take too much water from underground sources, the water may eventually run out. In hot, dry countries, and when there is a drought, conserving water supplies becomes even more important.

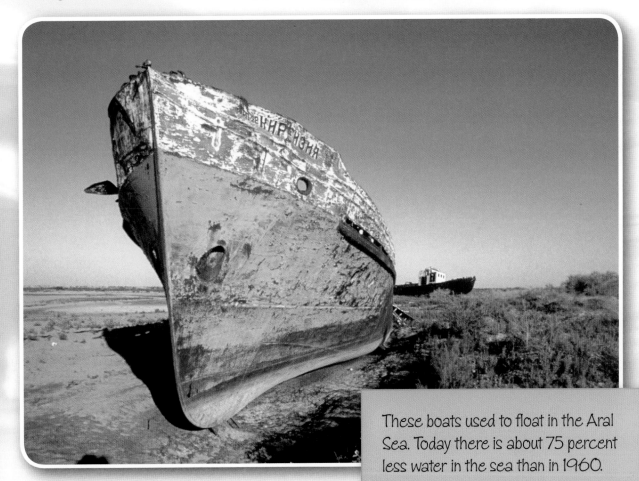

These boats used to float in the Aral Sea. Today there is about 75 percent less water in the sea than in 1960.

Harming the environment

Taking too much water from rivers and lakes can also harm the animals and plants that live there. Taking water changes the natural flow of a river. This can make it difficult for fish and other animals and plants to live in the river. Taking too much water from lakes and **wetlands** can make them shrink, leaving plants that grow around their edges without water.

How Much Water Do We Use?

Have you ever thought about how much water you use every day? It is probably a lot more than you think. We use water for drinking and washing. We also use it to prepare food and wash clothes and dishes. Huge amounts of water are used in factories to make the things we buy in the stores.

How much do I use at home?

In a **developed** country, an average person uses up to around 50 gallons (200 liters) of water a day indoors at home. That is enough to fill a bathtub full to the brim. Amazingly, most of this water is used for flushing the toilet. Added to this, you probably use about 6.5 gallons (25 liters) of water every day at school. People in hot, dry places use more water in their gardens.

Water helps keep you clean. It washes dirt from your hands and takes it away down the drain.

Taking Action: Keep a Water Diary

Figure out how much water you use by keeping a water diary. During the day, make a note every time you use some water. Write down what you used the water for and when you used it. If you use a tap, count the number of seconds the tap runs. Use the numbers below to figure out the total amount of water you used in the day.

Toilet flush:	3 gallons (12 liters) per flush
Running tap:	About 1 quart (1 litre) every ten seconds
Shower:	10 gallons (38 liters)
Bath:	20 gallons (76 liters)
Garden hose:	4 gallons (15 liters) per minute
Washing machine:	25 gallons (96 liters) per cycle

Who else uses water?

Farmers need lots of water for growing **crops**, especially when the weather is hot and dry. It takes more than 13 gallons (50 liters) of water to grow just one orange. Factories also use large quantities of water for processing **raw materials** and making things. For example, it takes about 2 gallons (8 liters) of water to make a newspaper.

We use billions of gallons of water every year to help crops grow.

Where Does Our Water Come From?

The water we use comes from three places. These are rivers, lakes, and rocks under the ground. Your water might come from just one of these places or from all three. Water gets into rivers, lakes, and rocks because of the water cycle. The water we use is on its way round the water cycle.

Science Behind It: The Water Cycle

The water cycle is the way in which Earth's water is used over and over again. Without the water cycle, we would have no freshwater. During the water cycle, water **evaporates** from the oceans into the **atmosphere**. Only the water evaporates, leaving the salt behind. In the atmosphere, the water **condenses** to form clouds. Water falls from the clouds as rain or snow. Some falls directly into rivers or the ocean. Some soaks into the ground or runs off into rivers and flows back to the ocean, where the cycle begins again.

The water cycle carries water from the oceans to land and back again.

Clouds form

Rain falls from clouds

Water evaporates

Rain flows into rivers and lakes

Lake

Rain soaks into the ground

Ocean

What is a reservoir?

A reservoir is an artificial (human-made) lake. Some reservoirs take water from rivers flowing along in deep valleys. A dam is built across the valley to catch the water. Then the water is stored in the reservoir until it is needed. Reservoirs also store water that is pumped out of rivers.

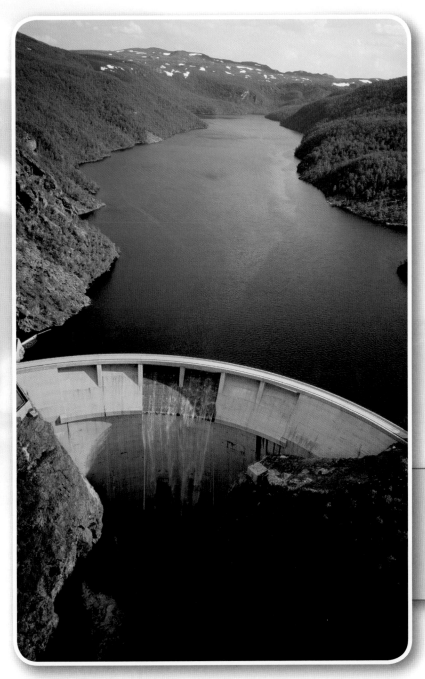

How is water stored underground?

Some rocks have lots of tiny spaces inside them. Water can trickle through these spaces. If the water cannot drain away, it fills the rock with water. Gradually, this builds up an underground supply of water. These water-filled rocks are called **aquifers**. We get water out of aquifers through wells drilled down into the rock.

A dam like this can hold enough water for a large town for several months.

11

How does water get to us?

Water comes to our schools, homes, offices, and factories along pipes under the ground. A wide pipe carries the water to towns and cities. Then smaller pipes carry the water along each street and to each building. Some buildings have a water tank in the roof to store water.

Many people in **developed countries** depend on a complex system of underground pipes to bring them water.

Is the water dirty?

Water taken from rivers, reservoirs, and aquifers can be dirty, so it is cleaned before we can use it. To do this, it is pumped to a **water treatment plant**. The water goes through a metal grill to remove any large pieces of trash. Then, chemicals are added to get dirt out and to kill any **microorganisms** living in the water. Finally, the water is tested to make sure that it is clean enough to drink.

Can we get water from the oceans?

It is possible to use water from the oceans, but first it must have the salt taken out to make it freshwater. This process is called **desalination**. Desalination plants (or factories) are built in places very far from any sources of freshwater. They boil the water, which leaves the salt behind. However, desalination uses up lots of energy. This makes the water very expensive.

Other ways people get water

Millions of people in the world do not have water piped to them. They cannot just turn on a tap to get their water. Instead, they get water from a well and carry it home in containers. They are very careful not to waste their water.

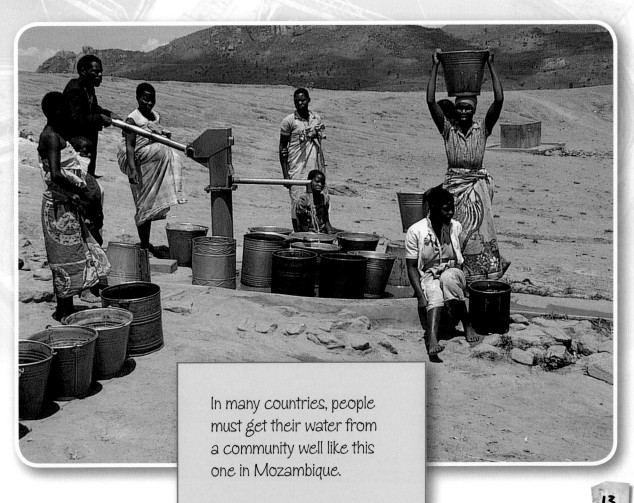

In many countries, people must get their water from a community well like this one in Mozambique.

13

What Happens to Waste Water?

What happens to all the dirty water that goes down the drain? What about the water that comes out of washing machines and that we flush down the toilet? The answer is that is goes back into rivers or the sea. But it is always cleaned first to remove any waste, dirt, and chemicals.

Water from a sink begins its long journey to the water treatment plant.

Where is dirty water cleaned?

Waste water flows into underground pipes called drains. It flows along the drains into large pipes, called **sewers**, under the streets. The sewers lead to a **water treatment plant**, where the water is cleaned. The clean water flows back into a river or flows along pipes out to the ocean.

How is waste water cleaned?

First, the dirty water is poured through a metal grill, like a sieve. This catches large items, such as twigs and plastic bags. Then the water flows slowly through large tanks, where smaller bits of sand and grit settle to the bottom. **Microorganisms** are added that eat waste and other harmful microorganisms. Now the water is clean. The dirt that has been removed from the water forms a sludge. The sludge is buried underground, used as **fertilizer**, or burned.

Water is cleaned by bacteria in these tanks.

Science Behind It: Bacteria Cleans Your Water

Bacteria are tiny microorganisms. Some bacteria are dangerous because they cause diseases. But some kinds of bacteria and other microorganisms called protozoa help clean dirty waste water. They eat waste in the water and other kinds of bacteria in the water that might cause disease.

Taking Action: Don't Pour Away Chemicals

Some chemicals, such as motor oil, paint, and weed killers, are difficult to remove from water. It is better not to pour them down the sink. Ask your family to store waste chemicals carefully, where they will not get spilled. Then ask an adult to help you find out where they can be disposed of safely.

How Can We Save Water at Home?

There are three simple ways of cutting the amount of water we use. First, we can waste less water. Second, we can collect rainwater and use it instead of tap water. Finally, we can reuse some water instead of pouring it down the drain.

Changing the washer on a dripping tap will save a lot of water.

How can I waste less water?

Huge amounts of water are just poured down the drain without being used for anything. This is a terrible waste. Here are some simple ways to stop wasting water:

- Don't let the tap run while you are brushing your teeth. Turn it off!
- Fill a basin or sink for washing in, instead of letting the water run.
- When you turn on the hot water, collect the cold water that comes out first. Use it to water houseplants or the garden.
- Use a dishwasher or washing machine only when you have a full load.

Does water leak away?

Lots of water is wasted because it leaks away through dripping taps or leaky toilet tanks. A dripping tap could waste 7 gallons (27 liters) of water a day! Check your home for dripping taps, and ask your family to replace the washers.

Taking Action: Use Water Efficiently

Save water by only using as much as you really need. One easy way is to take a quick shower instead of a bath. This could save more than 13 gallons (50 liters) of water a day. You can save a liter of water every time you flush the toilet by putting a liter bottle of water in the tank. When your parents buy a new washing machine or dishwasher, ask them to choose a model that uses water efficiently.

By taking up space in the tank, a bottle of water reduces the amount of water needed to fill it up again.

How can we save water outdoors?

Think of all the ways we use water outdoors. We water plants and lawns in the summer, and we use water for cleaning windows and cars. Here are some ways in which you can stop wasting so much water:

• Water plants and lawns in the evening to reduce **evaporation**.
• Put wood chips or straw on flowerbeds to reduce evaporation.
• Cut grass a bit longer than normal. This will keep the soil under the grass from drying out as quickly in hot weather.

Straw covers the soil, helping to keep the soil drying out. This means it needs less watering.

Science Behind It: Evaporating Water

Evaporation is the way in which liquid water turns into gas when it heats up. If you water your garden during the warm daytime, the water evaporates quickly. It is better to water the garden in the evening, when it is cooler, so evaporation happens more slowly. Then the water has time to soak into the ground.

How can we use rainwater?

You can use rainwater to water plants and lawns. The best way to collect rainwater is in a rain barrel. A rain barrel can be attached to a downspout to collect the rain that flows off your roof.

Where can we reuse water?

Reusing water means using waste water for another job instead of simply pouring it down the drain. For example, you can water the garden or houseplants with the water from cooking food, from washing vegetables, and from an inflatable swimming pool. Do not put soapy water on the garden because it could harm the plants.

A rain barrel like this can provide all the water your garden needs.

Taking Action: Trap Runoff

Runoff is rainwater that flows across the land and into streams and rivers. Runoff from your garden normally flows into drains, but you can trap runoff so that it soaks into the ground instead. Try some of these ideas out at home or at school. Ask permission from a parent or teacher first.

- Replace solid concrete paving stones with gravel. This will let water seep through into the ground.
- Build terraces in sloping flower beds so that water can soak into the soil before it drains away.
- Make a rain garden by digging a shallow hole in the ground. Water will collect in the dip, keeping the ground moist. Plants will grow better here than on dry ground.

How Can We Save Water at School?

At school, you use water for painting and washing, in the washrooms, in the locker room, and for drinking. Water is also used in the school kitchens and for watering the landscaping and playing fields. Saving water is good for the environment. It also saves money because your school has to pay for every drop of water it uses.

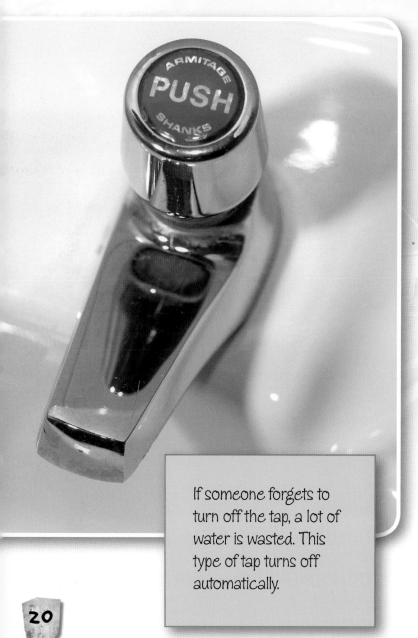

If someone forgets to turn off the tap, a lot of water is wasted. This type of tap turns off automatically.

How can we use less water?

A simple way to save water at school is to make sure you turn off any taps you use. Leaving them running wastes lots of water. Check that other students have turned off the taps, too. You could ask your school about putting in taps that turn off automatically. Your school could also put in toilets that flush automatically after each use. Ask about saving water in the school kitchens. Water used to prepare and cook vegetables could be reused to water your school's landscaping.

Taking Action: Water Watch!

Tell other students and teachers at your school about the importance of saving water by starting a water-watch **campaign**. Make posters for your campaign telling people about the problems of wasting water and suggesting simple ways for saving it. Make posters for the washrooms to remind students to turn off the taps. You could also do a presentation at a school assembly and on the school website.

Get your friends involved and see what you can do to help conserve water at your school!

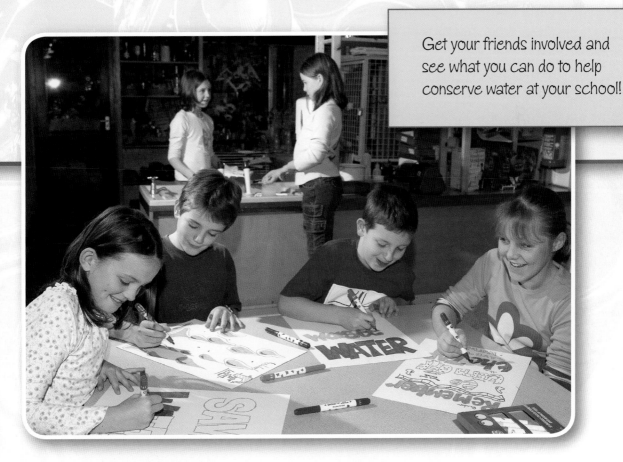

Rainwater harvesting

Some schools have a **rainwater harvesting** system. It is like a rain barrel, but more complicated. The system collects water that runs off the roof and stores it in a tank. The water is cleaned and used for flushing toilets and washing hands as well as watering landscaping and fields. This saves hundreds of gallons of water every day.

Case Study: Rainwater Harvesting in Delhi, India

The Shri Ram School is in Delhi, India. The school's main source of water is a well that goes down into an **aquifer**. The water is pumped from underground. The school also gets some water from the city's supply. In 2000, the water level in the well was dropping and the school was in danger of running out of water. So the school decided to put in a **rainwater harvesting** system.

In most rainwater harvesting systems, the water is stored in tanks above ground, but the school decided to use a system that would store water in the aquifer. Gutters collect the rainwater that flows off the school's roofs. Pipes carry the water to a large tank. Water from the tank trickles down a deep well into the aquifer under the ground.

The Shri Ram School system has been a great success. It collects millions of gallons of rainwater each year, much more than the students and staff need. Also, the water level in the aquifer has slowly risen again.

These girls are learning about a water system at their school in Bangladesh.

Why Is Clean Water So Important?

You probably take a supply of clean water for granted at home or school. You can turn on a tap and clean water comes flowing out. But millions of people in **developing** countries are not as lucky. They do not have clean water supplies. They have to use dirty water for drinking and washing because they have no choice.

Is dirty water dangerous?

If harmful chemicals and **microorganisms** get into the water supply, it can make the water very dangerous. Waste chemicals from factories can make people blind if they get into the water supply. Microorganisms such as **bacteria** cause diseases such as **cholera** and **typhoid**. Both of these diseases can kill people. More than five million people die every year from drinking dirty water.

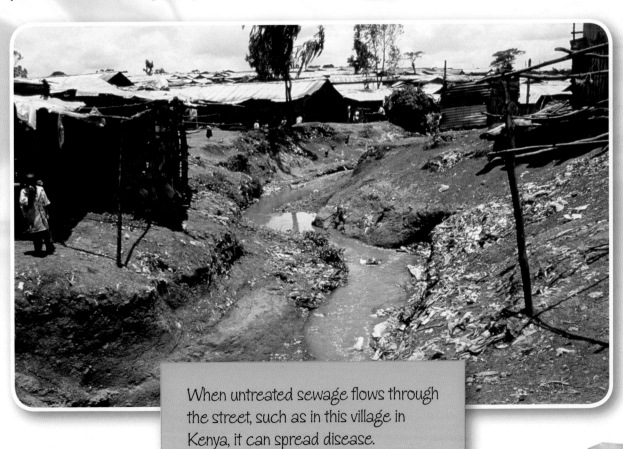

When untreated sewage flows through the street, such as in this village in Kenya, it can spread disease.

23

Science Behind It: Disease in the Water

Even water that looks clean can cause diseases if it contains microorganisms such as bacteria. These bacteria are so small you can only see them with a microscope. Many sorts of bacteria are harmless. In fact, you have millions of harmless bacteria living in your body. But some bacteria make us ill if they get inside our bodies, because they make poisonous chemicals. Our water supply is tested to make sure it is free of harmful microorganisms.

These tiny cholera bacteria (seen through a microscope) can cause a very serious disease.

Taking Action: Raising Money To Help

Ask a parent or teacher to help you research organizations that help people in developing countries find ways to make their water supplies safer. Then, arrange a sponsored walk or swim to raise money for the organization.

What makes water dirty?

If you are lucky enough to have a supply of clean water, you must take care of it. Having a dirty, **polluted** water supply is as bad as having no water at all. It is very important to keep our precious water supplies as clean as possible. This means that we must not pollute the water in our rivers and **aquifers**. Things that pollute water include human waste, factory chemicals, and farm chemicals. River pollution not only harms people but also animals and plants that live in the river.

Factories are one source of pollution in rivers and streams. This water is called industrial effluent.

Waste water pollution

Sometimes rivers become polluted because waste water flows into them without being cleaned first. The water may contain human waste, chemicals, and litter. In some places, the water is not treated because there is no sewage system and no **water treatment plant**. It flows straight from homes into rivers, lakes, or the oceans.

Science Behind It: Plant Blooms

Fertilizers, animal waste, and **detergents** contain two chemicals called phosphorus and nitrogen. They are often washed into streams and rivers when it rains. The phosphorus and nitrogen make plants in the river grow very quickly. When the plants die, bacteria start rotting them. Bacteria use up lots of **oxygen** from the water. Then there is less oxygen left for fish and other animals, so they may die.

This water is full of a type of plant called algae.

Taking Action: Pollution Watch

Carry out a pollution check on your local stream. Looking at live animals in the water, such as fish, insects, and shrimps, is a good way to check how polluted a stream is. Ask an adult to help you with your study. Use a jar to collect a sample of water. Examine the water with a magnifying glass. If you see many small animals, the water is probably very clean.

Case Study: Cleaning Up the River Thames

At one time, the River Thames in London, England, was one of the dirtiest rivers in the world. In the early 1800s, London's population grew to more than a million as people moved into the city from the countryside. There were no water pipes or **sewers**. The people got their water straight from the Thames and put their waste water straight back into the river.

The river became very dirty and by the 1850s, it was like a giant sewer! No animals or plants could live in the water, and the smell was terrible. Many people died from **cholera** because they drank the dirty water.

DIPHTHERIA   SCROFULA   CHOLERA

FATHER THAMES INTRODUCES HIS OFFSPRING TO THE FAIR CITY OF LONDON
(A Design for a Fresco in the New Houses of Parliament.)

This picture shows what people in the 1800s thought of the filthy river.

The Thames became cleaner when sewers were put in, but it was filthy again by the 1960s. Then, modern **water treatment plants** were built, and the river began to get cleaner. Fish began to return and in 1974, a salmon was caught in London. It was the first salmon caught there in 140 years! Since then the water has continued to get cleaner.

Fact File

- The average person in the United States uses about 50 gallons (about 200 liters) of water per day. The average person in Africa uses about about 2 gallons (about 7 liters) of water per day.
- On average, nearly a tenth of all the water piped to homes is lost because of leaks.
- In Australia between 35 and 50 percent of all water used at home is used to water gardens.
- In the USA more than 145 trillion gallons (550 trillion liters) of water is taken out of rivers and **aquifers** every year. Much of this is used for watering **crops**.
- About 90 percent of all the water we take goes down the drain afterward. The rest gets drunk or goes on the garden.
- About 40 percent of the drinking water supply in the United States comes from underground aquifers.
- In your lifetime you will use more than a swimming pool full of water for flushing the toilet.

further Reading

Ball, Jackie. *Conservation and Natural Resources*. Milwaukee, Wisc.: Gareth Stevens Publishing, 2004.

Graham, Ian. *Water: A Resource Our World Depends On*. Chicago: Heinemann Library, 2004.

Stefanow, Jennifer. *Polluted Waters*. Chicago: Raintree, 2004.

Glossary

aquifer layer of underground rocks filled with water

atmosphere layer of air that surrounds Earth

bacteria tiny living things that live in air, water, or soil

campaign series of things done by a group of people to achieve a result

cholera disease caused by bacteria that infect the intestines

condense turn from gas to liquid

crop plant grown by farmers for food

desalination removal of salt from salt water (for example ocean water)

detergent chemical used for cleaning

developed describes a country that has advanced industries and where most people have an education, jobs, a place to live, and food to eat

developing describes a country where many people do not have much money and do not have much education. Such countries often have food shortages, few sources of power, and poor transportation systems.

drought long period of time without rain

evaporate turn from liquid to gas, but at a temperature lower than the liquid's boiling point

fertilizer chemical that helps plants grow

microorganism plant, animal or other living thing that is too small to see with the naked eye

oxygen one of the gases in the air that animals need to breathe to stay alive

pollution something that makes air, water, or other parts of Earth's environment dirty

rainwater harvesting collecting rainwater so we can use it. This means we take less water from the mains water supply.

30

raw material material we get from the Earth in its natural state, which we can then use to make other things

resource anything that is useful to people

sewer pipe under the ground that carries dirty water to a water treatment plant

terrace area on a slope that has been made level

typhoid disease caused by bacteria that may cause death. Typhoid is spread when people eat food or drink water that has the bacteria in it.

water treatment plant place where dirty water is cleaned before it goes back into rivers or the sea

wetland area of land, such as a marsh or a swamp, that is normally covered with a shallow layer of water

Index